I0813651

ANIMAL SHOWDOWNS

ARCTIC FOX VS. RED FOX

by Cynthia O'Brien

Kaleidoscope
Minneapolis, MN

The Quest for Discovery Never Ends

This edition first published in 2025 by Kaleidoscope Publishing, Inc.

For information regarding permission, write to
Kaleidoscope Publishing, Inc.
6012 Blue Circle Drive
Minnetonka, MN 55343

Library of Congress Control Number
2024935963

ISBN
978-1-64519-793-5 (library bound)
978-1-64519-841-3 (ebook)

Developed by Focus Strategic Communications Inc.

Printed in the United States of America.

Precious McKenzie, Developmental Editor

Bigfoot lurks within one of the images in this book. It's up to you to find him!

TABLE OF CONTENTS

Chapter 1

Fox Fight

Hello animal lovers, and welcome to the ANIMAL SHOWDOWNS series. Today, two clever hunters will try to outsmart each other. Which fox has the better moves? Will size and strength decide the match?

Arctic fox
Species:
Vulpes lagopus

It is still snowy and cold in the **tundra**. The Arctic fox stops and perks up his ears. He has been hunting for a long time and hears a lemming moving under the snow. In the winter, these small **rodents** are the fox's main prey. The Arctic fox peers across the snow. He spots a red fox.

The two foxes are cousins, but they are not friends. Right now, the red fox is looking for food, too. He has his eyes on the Arctic fox. The fox fight is about to begin.

Red fox
Species: Vulpes vulpes

Usually, foxes hunt small animals such as lemmings and squirrels. They also eat plants, birds, and eggs. In the winter, food can be hard to find. Arctic foxes follow polar bears. The fox waits until the polar bear has caught a seal in the icy Arctic Ocean. After the bear eats and leaves, the fox eats what is left behind.

Sometimes, red foxes attack and eat other foxes. This includes the Arctic fox.

FUN FACT
The Arctic fox gathers food in the summer and stores it for the winter.

The Arctic fox still wants to catch the lemming, but the red fox watches him. They are both still.

Suddenly, the Arctic fox leaps up and then dives down into the snow headfirst. He pokes his head up. No luck this time. The lemming escaped.

The red fox lunges towards the Arctic fox. He bites at the Arctic fox's tail, ripping off some fur.

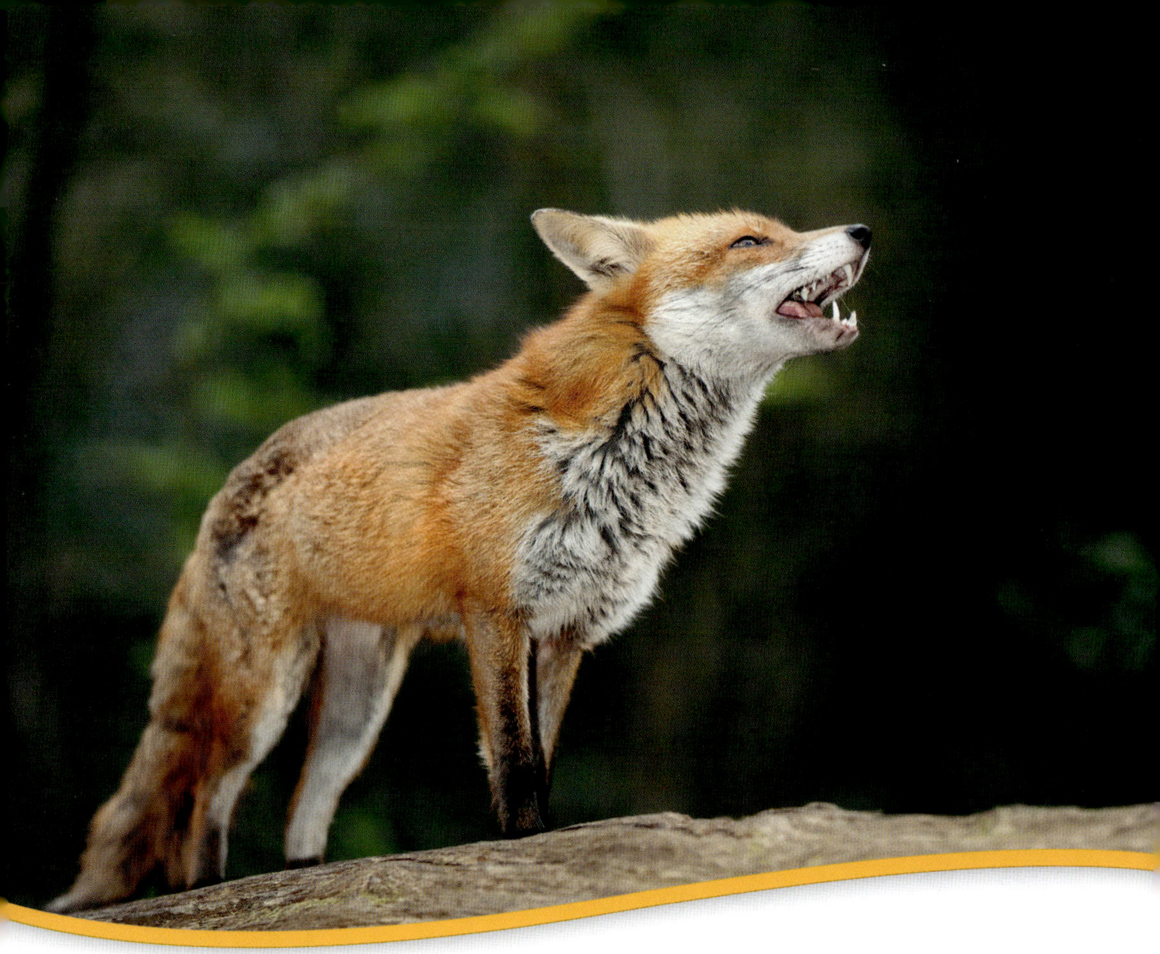

The Arctic fox is not hurt. His tail is covered in thick fur. He screams at the red fox. Foxes scream when they are angry. They also scream to warn other animals to stay away. The red fox is more **aggressive** than the Arctic fox and he is not afraid. He barks loudly at the Arctic fox.

SCOREBOARD

	ROUND 2 SCORE	TOTAL SCORE
Arctic Fox	3	3
Red Fox	3	11

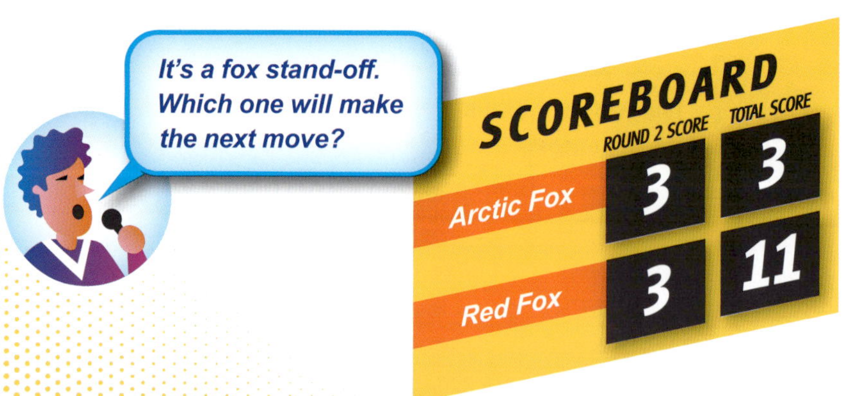

Foxes are related to dogs and wolves. They are part of the canine family. Arctic foxes are smaller than red foxes. They are about the size of a large house cat.

Size Comparison

ARCTIC FOX
Length: 18–26 inches (45–85 centimeters)
Tail Length: Up to 13 inches (30 centimeters)
Weight: 6.5 to 17 pounds (3–7.5 kilograms)

RED FOX
Length: 18 to 33 inches (45–85 centimeters)
Tail Length: 12 to 21 inches (30–53 centimeters)
Weight: 6.5 to 24 pounds (3–11 kilograms)

FOX TAILS

Foxes have long, bushy tails. Their tails help them to balance as they walk or run. When it is cold, foxes also wrap their tails around their bodies. This is just like a warm fluffy blanket.

FUN FACT

Fox tails are also called brushes.

Chapter 2

Who Invited You?

Climate change is making Earth warmer. This causes many problems for Arctic animals. They lose food. The ice is melting and changing their home. Other animals, such as the red fox, are moving north.

The Arctic fox does not like having the red fox around. Both animals hunt for the same food. Red foxes take over **dens** that Arctic foxes call home. The red fox is also dangerous.

The red fox leaps toward the Arctic fox again, but he darts away just in time.

And the chase is on. The red fox gets a few points for starting the race, even though the Arctic fox runs away.

SCOREBOARD

	ROUND 3 SCORE	TOTAL SCORE
Arctic Fox	8	11
Red Fox	3	14

Both foxes can run about 31 miles (50 kilometers) per hour for a short time. The Arctic fox has **adapted** to his chilly home. He is used to running in the snow. Will this help him in his race with the red fox?

FURRY FEET

The red fox and Arctic fox have fur on their feet. An Arctic fox's fur is thick and helps it to move through the snow and to keep warm. The Arctic fox's scientific name, "lagopus," means "rabbit-footed."

Arctic Fox

short, rounded ears

small, short (pointed) snout

whiskers

short legs

fur-covered feet

long, thick tail

long, white-tipped tail

Red Fox

FUN FACT
Red foxes can also have brown, black, and silver fur.
pointed black ears
reddish-brown fur
pointed snout
whiskers
white chest and chin
black legs
black feet
short claws

Where Do ARCTIC FOXES AND RED FOXES *Live?*

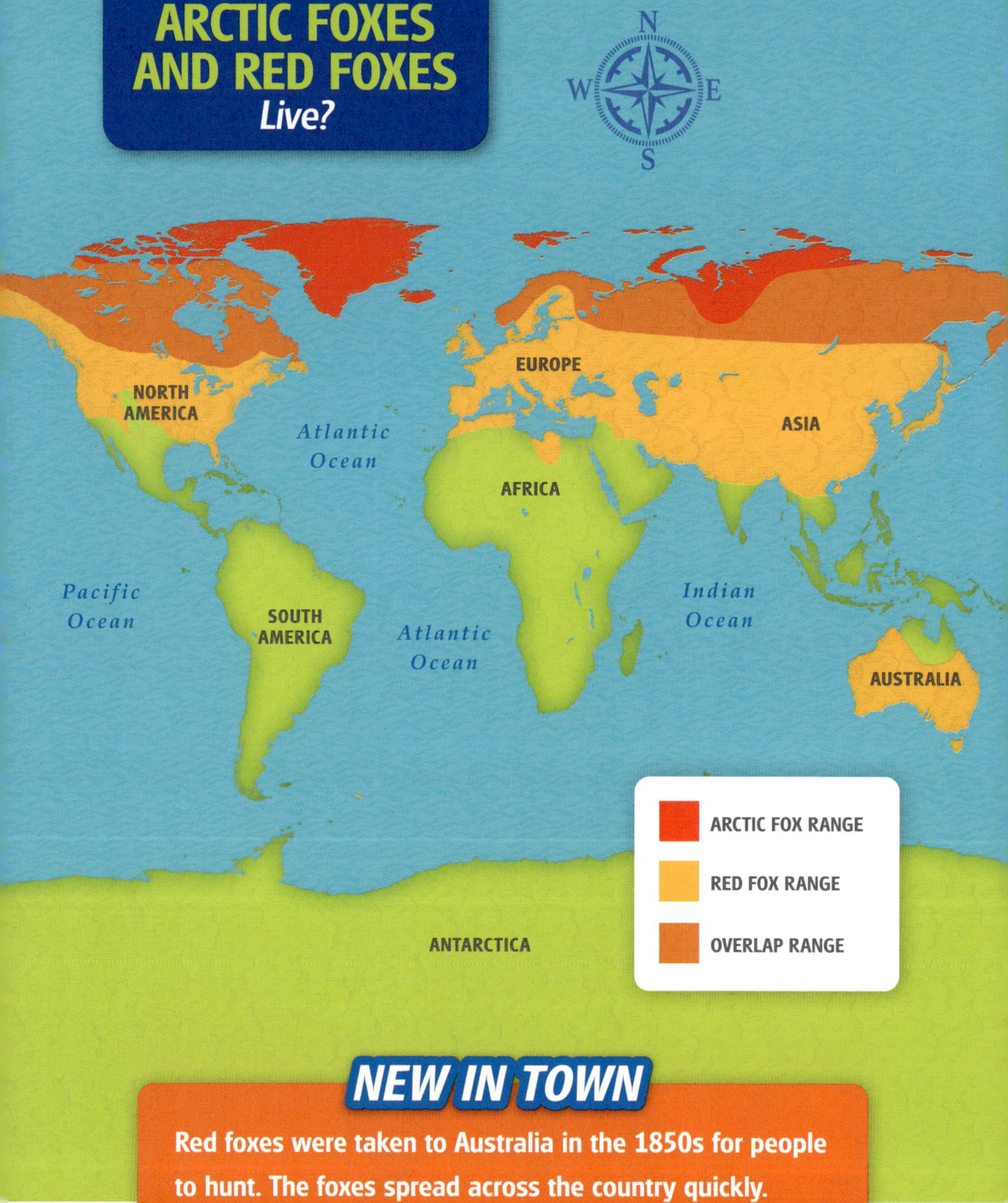

NORTH AMERICA

Atlantic Ocean

EUROPE

ASIA

AFRICA

Pacific Ocean

SOUTH AMERICA

Atlantic Ocean

Indian Ocean

AUSTRALIA

ANTARCTICA

ARCTIC FOX RANGE

RED FOX RANGE

OVERLAP RANGE

NEW IN TOWN

Red foxes were taken to Australia in the 1850s for people to hunt. The foxes spread across the country quickly. Today, red foxes live in most parts of Australia.

CHANGING COLOR

The Arctic fox has white fur during the winter. This helps to camouflage it in the snow. Animals such as Arctic wolves and polar bears sometimes hunt the Arctic fox. In the summer, the Arctic fox sheds its heavy white fur. Its summer fur is brown. This helps to camouflage it from predators against the rocks and land. A few Arctic foxes have a blue-tinted fur coat. These foxes mainly live near the sea.

FUN FACT

The Arctic fox has the warmest fur of any animal in the Arctic.

Chapter 3

Catch Me If You Can!

The Arctic fox runs toward his den. He is a blur of white. The red fox stops still, not having seen him enter the den. He listens and can hear another lemming under the snow. Patiently he waits, wanting to pounce on the right spot.

He dives on the lemming and grabs the small rodent. This keeps him busy for a while.

Points to the Arctic fox for his quick getaway. How long can he hide from the red fox?

SCOREBOARD

	ROUND 4 SCORE	TOTAL SCORE
Arctic Fox	5	16
Red Fox	0	14

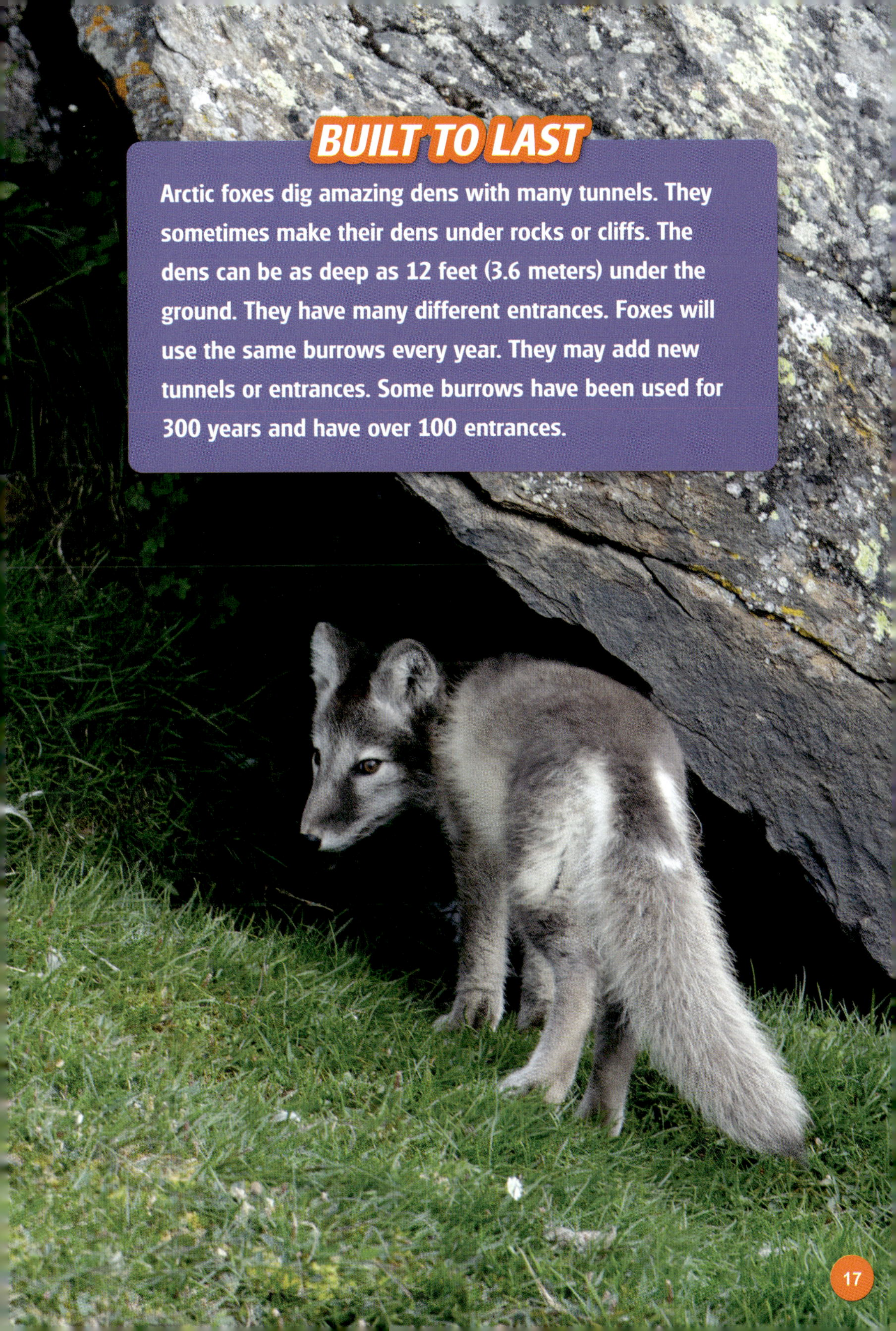

BUILT TO LAST

Arctic foxes dig amazing dens with many tunnels. They sometimes make their dens under rocks or cliffs. The dens can be as deep as 12 feet (3.6 meters) under the ground. They have many different entrances. Foxes will use the same burrows every year. They may add new tunnels or entrances. Some burrows have been used for 300 years and have over 100 entrances.

The red fox is finished with the lemming. He spots the den and sniffs around the outside. Which entrance should he take? He picks one and rushes inside. The Arctic fox tries to hide as the red fox stops and listens. His whiskers tingle. He hears a soft noise.

The Arctic fox tries to get out through another entrance, but the red fox pounces. His sharp claws dig into the Arctic fox's fur. The Arctic fox yelps. He runs out of the den. The red fox is right behind him.

SUPER SENSES

Foxes can twist their ears around to pick up sounds. This helps them to know exactly where a noise is coming from.

Fennec fox

BIG FAMILY

There are twelve different species of foxes that are considered "true" foxes. The true foxes include the red fox and the Arctic fox. Each fox has adapted to its habitat. Fennec foxes are the smallest foxes in the world. They have large ears and live in deserts in Africa. Tibetan foxes live in high, rocky areas in Asia. They have yellowish gray fur. This helps to camouflage them from predators and prey. Other foxlike animals are not true foxes. These include bat-eared foxes and gray foxes.

Tibetan fox

A TOOTHY GRIN

Foxes have 42 teeth, which include four sharp teeth called canines. These pointed teeth help foxes to kill other animals. Foxes do not chew their food. They tear it apart with their teeth and then swallow it.

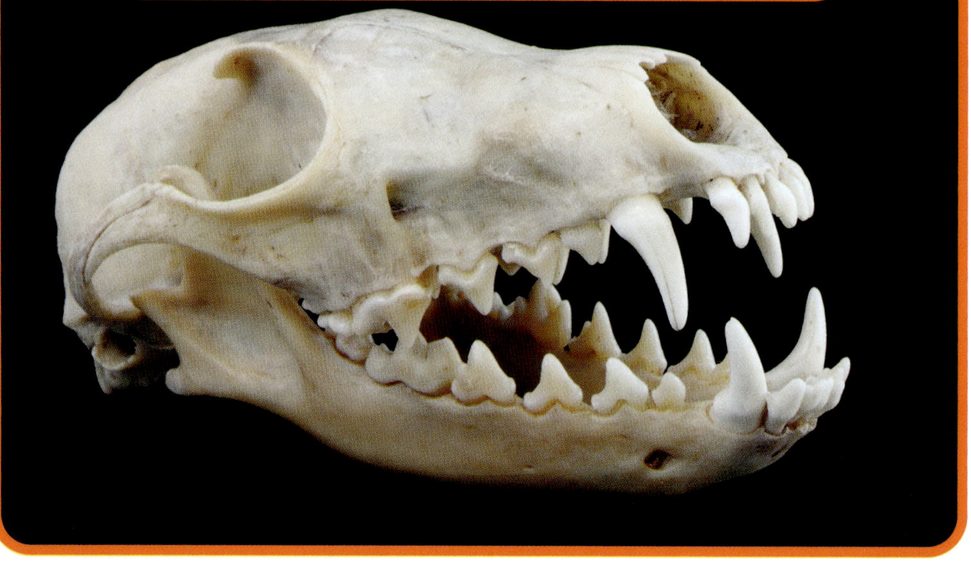

The red fox snaps at the Arctic fox. Again, the Arctic fox's thick fur helps to protect him. The Arctic fox turns and bites back. He bites into the red fox's side, making a big wound. The fox starts to bleed.

SCOREBOARD

	ROUND 6 SCORE	TOTAL SCORE
Arctic Fox	10	29
Red Fox	5	29

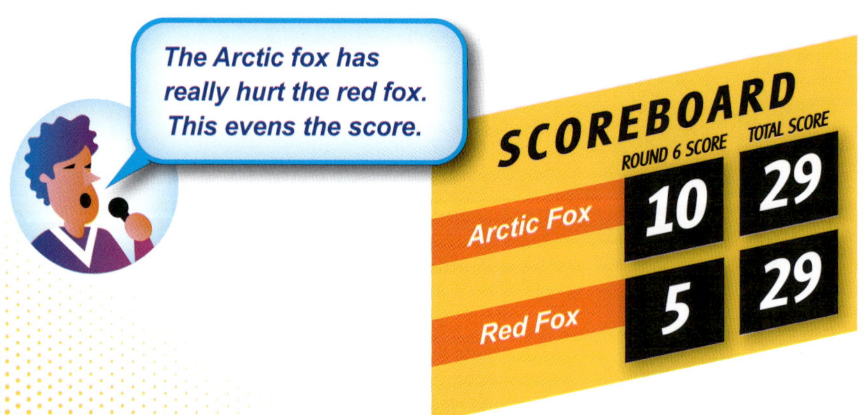

Now the red fox is very angry. He is in pain and claws at the Arctic fox. This time, he digs through the fur and into the skin. He tries to pin the Arctic fox to the ground. The Arctic fox hits and scratches at the red fox.

Chapter 4

Trapped!

The Arctic fox uses all his strength to get away from the red fox. He shakes his body and screams. The red fox growls back. Both foxes stare into each other's eyes. In a flash, the red fox pounces again. He claws at the Arctic fox, but he does not push him down.

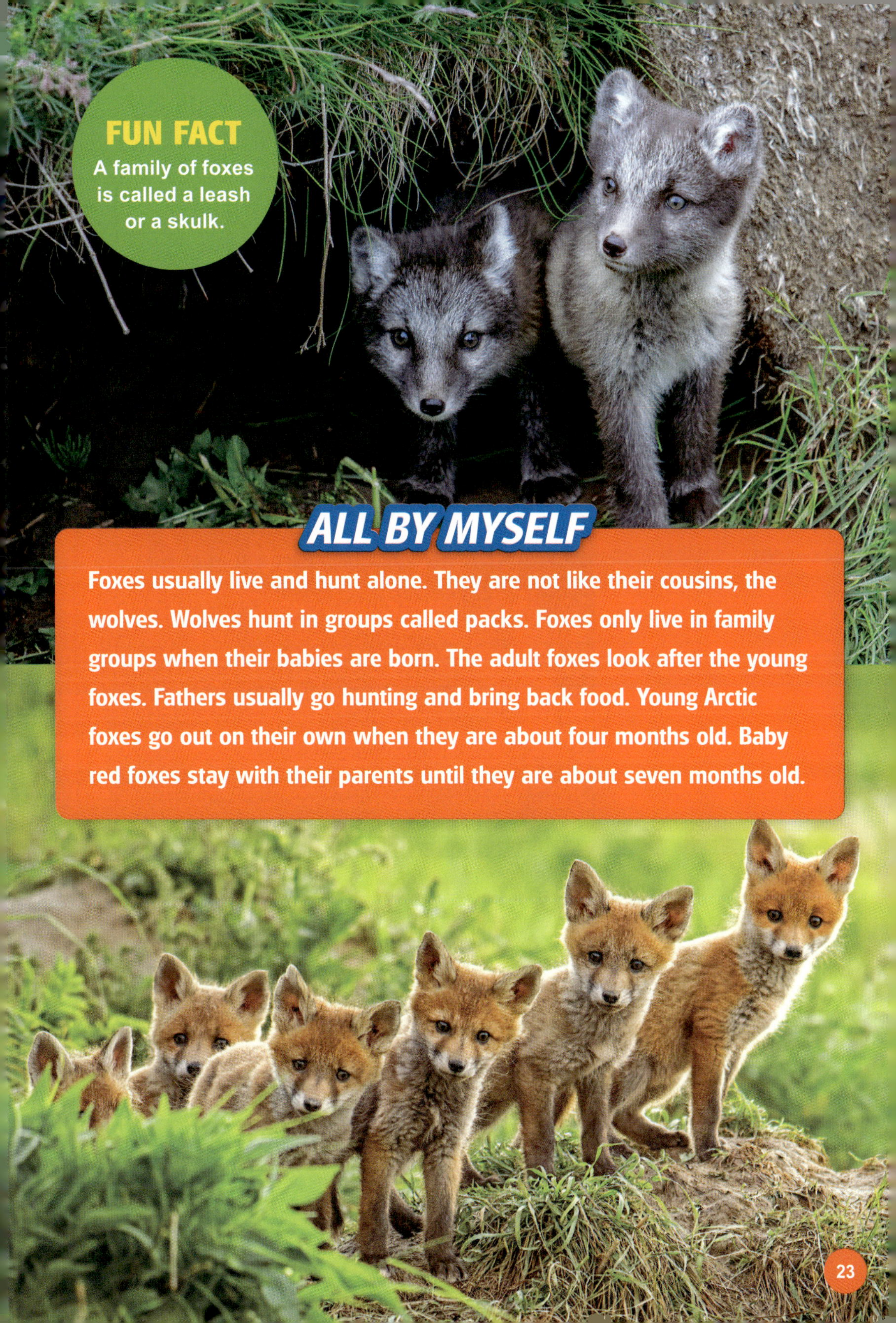

FUN FACT
A family of foxes is called a leash or a skulk.

ALL BY MYSELF

Foxes usually live and hunt alone. They are not like their cousins, the wolves. Wolves hunt in groups called packs. Foxes only live in family groups when their babies are born. The adult foxes look after the young foxes. Fathers usually go hunting and bring back food. Young Arctic foxes go out on their own when they are about four months old. Baby red foxes stay with their parents until they are about seven months old.

The Arctic fox tries to bite the red fox, but he misses the mark. He swipes his paws at the red fox instead, trying to push the bigger fox away. The red fox uses his body to push the Arctic fox down. This time, the Arctic fox is trapped. The red fox has pinned him to the ground.

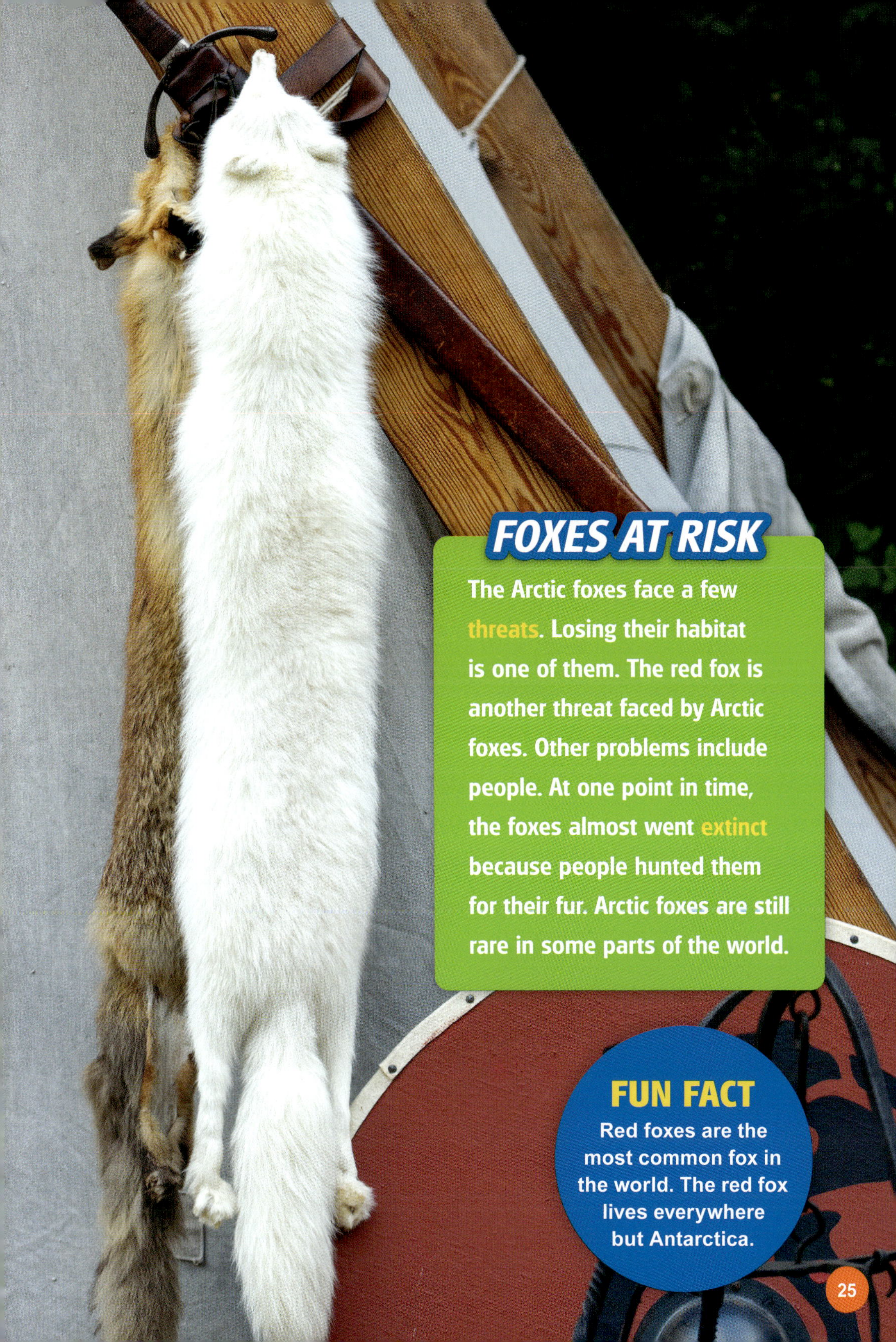

FOXES AT RISK

The Arctic foxes face a few threats. Losing their habitat is one of them. The red fox is another threat faced by Arctic foxes. Other problems include people. At one point in time, the foxes almost went extinct because people hunted them for their fur. Arctic foxes are still rare in some parts of the world.

FUN FACT

Red foxes are the most common fox in the world. The red fox lives everywhere but Antarctica.

The red fox has the Arctic fox exactly where he wants him. He just needs to take one last bite of the Arctic fox's neck.

The red fox has won the battle in the snowy Arctic wilderness. Next, he will move into the Arctic fox's den with the female fox. Their babies will be born in April or May. The red fox family will spend the summer together.

THINK ABOUT IT:

Could the Arctic fox have used other tricks to beat or escape the larger red fox?

After reading the book, it's time to think about what you learned. Try the following exercises to jumpstart your ideas.

THINK

FIND OUT MORE. There is so much more to dig up about Arctic foxes and red foxes. What do you want to learn? Look them up on the web, or check out a book from the library. Maybe even visit them at the zoo!

CREATE

ART TIME. Can you draw an Arctic fox or a red fox? Look up a picture and grab some markers and paper. Will your Arctic fox or red fox be in its habitat? What will it be doing? Will it be with another animal? The sky is the limit!

SHARE

THE MORE WHO KNOW. Share what you learned about Arctic foxes and red foxes. Use your own words to write a paragraph. What are the main ideas of this book? What facts from the book can you use to support those ideas? Share your paragraph with a classmate. Do they have any comments or questions?

GROW

HELP OUT! Many animals around the world are struggling to survive. Find an organization that is trying to save your favorite animal. Can you volunteer? Can your family donate to the organization's mission? You can also help by telling people about the animal. The more people who help, the safer the animal will be.

RESEARCH NINJA

Visit www.ninjaresearcher.com/7935 to learn how to take your research skills and book report writing to the next level!

Research

SEARCH LIKE A PRO

Learn how to use search engines to find useful websites.

FACT OR FAKE

Discover how you can tell a trusted website from an untrustworthy resource.

TEXT DETECTIVE

Explore how to zero in on the information you need most.

SHOW YOUR WORK

Research responsibly—learn how to cite sources.

Write

GET TO THE POINT

Learn how to express your main ideas.

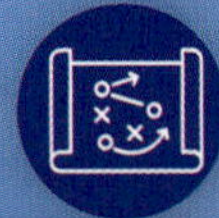

PLAN OF ATTACK

Learn prewriting exercises and create an outline.

Further Resources

BOOKS

Alkire, Jessie. *Arctic Foxes*. Edina, MN: ABDO, 2018.

Marie, Renata. *Arctic Foxes*. Minneapolis, MN: Kaleidoscope, 2023.

Orr, Nicole. *Red Foxes*. Mount Joy, PA: Fox Chapel Publishing, 2024.

WEBSITES

Factsurfer.com gives you a safe, fun way to find more information.

1. Go to www.factsurfer.com.
2. Enter "Arctic Fox vs. Red Fox" into the search box and click 🔍.
3. Select your book cover to see a list of related websites.

adapted: Changed or became used to an environment. Arctic foxes have adapted to living in the extreme cold.

aggressive: Forceful and ready to argue or attack others. The red fox is more aggressive than the Arctic fox.

climate change: The change in weather over a long period of time. Climate change is causing the Arctic ice to melt.

dens: Shelters for a wild animal. Arctic foxes use their dens to shelter from a snowstorm.

extinct: No longer existing. Dinosaurs are extinct.

camouflage: An animal's coloring that blends in with its surroundings. The Arctic fox's white fur helps to camouflage it in the snow.

habitat: The place where an animal or plant usually lives. Red foxes live in different kinds of habitats, including the tundra.

rodents: Small mammals with sharp front teeth. Lemmings and mice are rodents.

threats: Dangers or possible harms. The Arctic fox faces threats of red fox moving north due to increased temperatures.

tundra: Dry, cold, treeless areas of Earth. The tundra is found at the tops of very high mountains, in the Arctic, and in parts of Antarctica.

Index

PHOTO CREDITS

The images in this book are reproduced through the courtesy of: AB Photographie (Red fox); Alexey Seafarer (Arctic fox)/Shutterstock Images, cover; Eric Isselee/Shutterstock Images, p. 3; Sam Chadwick/Shutterstock Images, p. 4–5 (Arctic fox); Mark Caunt/Shutterstock Images, p. 4–5 (Red fox); pamas/Shutterstock Images, p. 4–5 (background); rooh183/Shutterstock Images, p. 6; Alexey Seafarer/Shutterstock Images, p. 7; Giedriius/Shutterstock Images, p. 8; Eric Isselee/Shutterstock Images, p. 9 (Arctic fox silhouette); Jim Cumming/Shutterstock Images, p. 9 (Red fox silhouette); Alexey Seafarer/Shutterstock Images, p. 9 (bottom); L-N/Shutterstock Images, p. 10; Alexey Seafarer/Shutterstock Images, p. 11 (top circle); Andrei Stepanov/Shutterstock Images, p. 11 (bottom circle); Jim Cumming/Shutterstock Images, p. 12–13 (Arctic fox); Jim Cumming/Shutterstock Images, p. 12–13 (Red fox); BlueBarronPhoto/Shutterstock Images, p. 13 (circle); Nicram Sabod/Shutterstock Images, p. 15; NaturesMomentsuk/Shutterstock Images, p. 16; Charles Bergman/Shutterstock Images, p. 17; Cecilie Bergan Stuedal/Shutterstock Images, p. 18; Artush/Shutterstock Images, p. 19 (top); han longwei/Shutterstock Images, p. 19 (bottom); photowind/Shutterstock Images, p. 20; L Galbraith/Shutterstock Images, p. 21; AngelaLouwe/Shutterstock Images, p. 22; Michael Zech Fotografie/Shutterstock Images, p. 23 (top); WildMedia/Shutterstock Images, p. 23 (bottom); Evelyn D. Harrison/Shutterstock Images, p. 24; LGieger/Shutterstock Images, p. 25; Rejean Aline Bedard/Shutterstock Images, p. 26–27; Jim Cumming/Shutterstock Images, p. 30.

About the Author

Cynthia O’Brien lives in Canada where she has listened to wolves howl, watched mountain goats climb, and peeked at bears fishing in the river. She loves to learn and write about the amazing animals that live all around the world.